MR. RHEE'S BRILLIANT
MATH SERIES

PRACTICE TESTS FOR

N N A T® 2

G R A D E   1

L E V E L   B

By Brian Rhee

2 Full-Length Practice Tests

70 Full Color Pages

Legal Notice

NNAT® Naglieri Nonverbal Ability Test was not involved in the production of this publication nor endorses this book.

Copyright © 2017 by Solomon Academy
Published by: Solomon Academy
First Edition
ISBN-13: 978-1545398890
ISBN-10: 1545398895

All rights reserved. This publication or any portion thereof may not be copied, replicated, distributed, or transmitted in any form or by any means whether electronically or mechanically whatsoever. It is illegal to produce derivative works from this publication, in whole or in part, without the prior written permission of the publisher and author.

Acknowledgements

I wish to acknowledge my deepest appreciation to my wife, Sookyung, who has continuously given me wholehearted support, encouragement, and love. Without you, I could not have completed this book.

Thank you to my sons, Joshua and Jason, who have given me big smiles and inspiration. I love you all.

About Author

Brian(Yeon) Rhee obtained a Masters of Arts Degree in Statistics at Columbia University, NY. He served as the Mathematical Statistician at the Bureau of Labor Statistics, DC. He is the Head Academic Director at Solomon Academy due to his devotion to the community coupled with his passion for teaching. His mission is to help students of all confidence level excel in academia to build a strong foundation in character, knowledge, and wisdom. Now, Solomon academy is known as the best academy specialized in Math in Northern Virginia.

Brian Rhee has published eight books which are available at www.amazon.com. The titles of his books are AP Calculus, SAT 1 Math, SAT 2 Math level 2, SHSAT/TJHSST Math workbook, IAAT (Iowa Algebra Aptitude Test) volume 1 and volume 2, CogAT form 7 level 8(Grade 2), and NNAT 2 level B(Grade 1). He's currently working on other math books which will be introduced in the near future.

Brian Rhee has twenty years of teaching experience in math. He has been one of the most popular tutors among TJHSST (Thomas Jefferson High School For Science and Technology) students. Currently, he is developing many online math courses with www.masterprep.net for AP Calculus AB and BC, SAT 2 Math level 2 test, SSAT/SHSAT, American Math Competitions such as AMC 10 and AMC 12, and other various math subjects.

About This Book

This book is designed towards mastering the NNAT® 2 from which many school districts identify gifted children for admissions into their gifted and talented programs. The book has 2 full-length (colored) practice tests and contains 70 full color pages. It provides a tool for a child to familiarize the format of the NNAT 2 Test without the use of any language.

About Naglieri Nonverbal Ability Test

The Naglieri Nonverbal Ability Test (NNAT®) is developed by Pearson Inc. The NNAT® is a multiple choice test and is used to measure the general ability of students ages 5 to 17. The Many school districts use the NNAT® to identify gifted children for admissions into their gifted and talented programs.

The questions on the NNAT® consists of geometric figures and shapes. A child needs to use reasoning and logical thinking to choose the answers. The NNAT® does not require a child to be able to read, write or speak in English.

The second edition of the NNAT®, known as NNAT2, consists of 3 sections: Pattern completion, reasoning by analogy, and serial reasoning. NNAT2 has 48 questions and takes 30 minutes to administer.

Section	Number of Questions
Pattern Completion	24
Reasoning by Analogy	12
Serial Reasoning	12

PRACTICE

TEST 1

Pattern Completion

> **Directions:** In the pattern completion section, each question has a large rectangle with a design. There is a small rectangle with a question mark that hides part of the design. Choose the answer that best completes the design.

Below is an example pattern completion question:

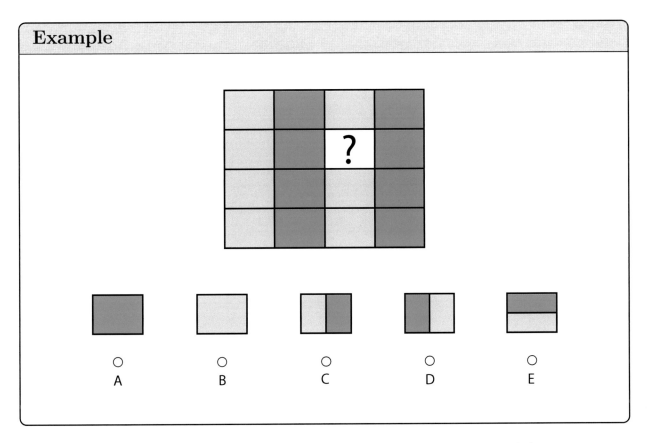

Example

In this example, the figure in (B) best completes the design. Therefore, (B) is the correct answer.

Question 1

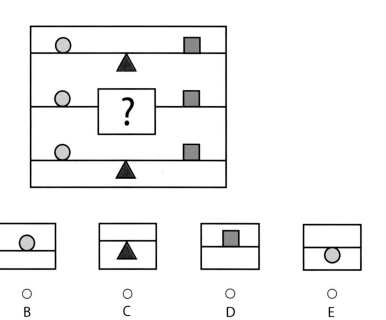

Question 2

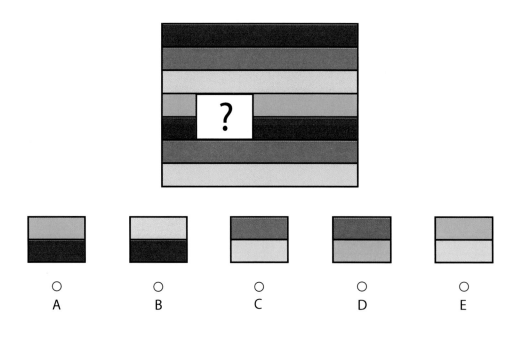

Question 3

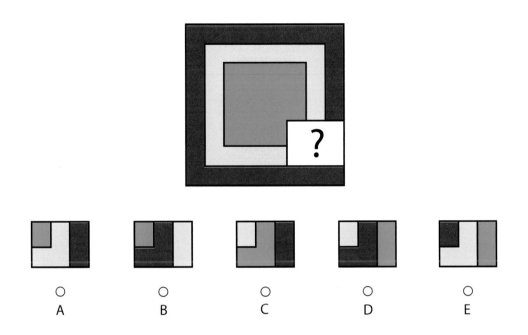

Question 4

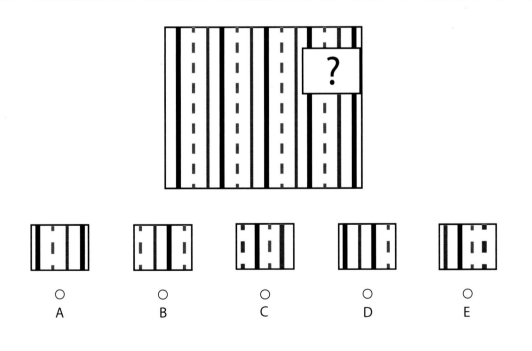

Question 5

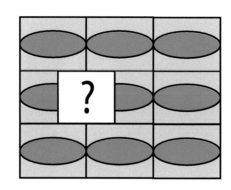

A   B   C   D   E

Question 6

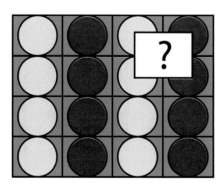

A   B   C   D   E

Question 7

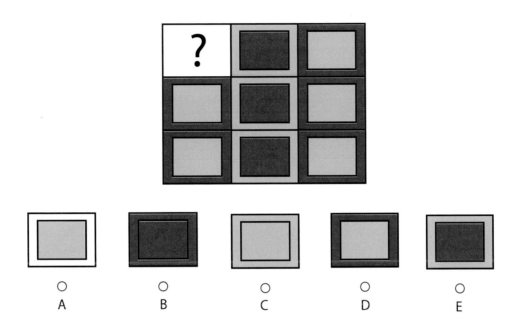

Question 8

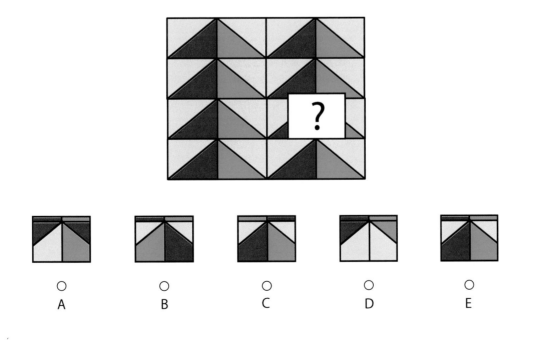

Question 9

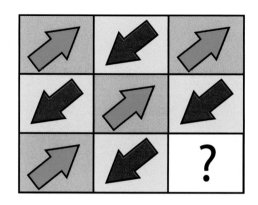

   ○   ○   ○   ○   ○

   A   B   C   D   E

Question 10

   ○   ○   ○   ○   ○

   A   B   C   D   E

Question 11

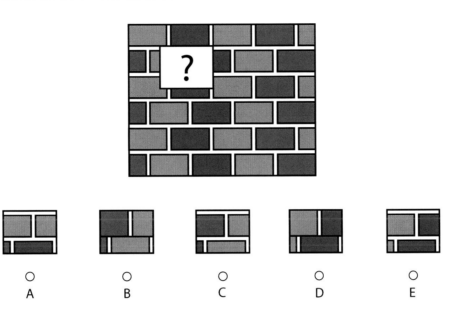

    ○   ○   ○   ○   ○

    A   B   C   D   E

Question 12

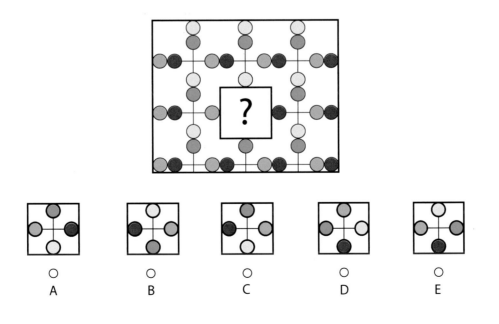

    ○   ○   ○   ○   ○

    A   B   C   D   E

Question 13

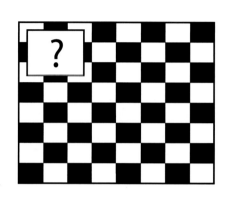

○   ○   ○   ○   ○
A   B   C   D   E

Question 14

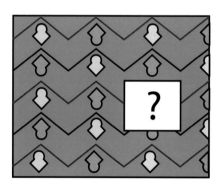

○   ○   ○   ○   ○
A   B   C   D   E

Question 15

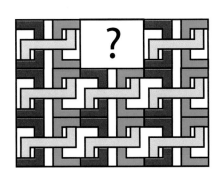

○ A   ○ B   ○ C   ○ D   ○ E

Question 16

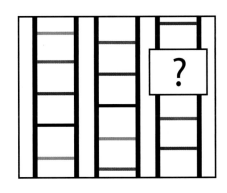

○ A   ○ B   ○ C   ○ D   ○ E

Question 17

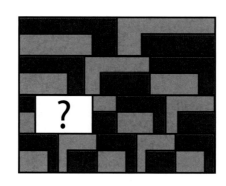

○   ○   ○   ○   ○
A   B   C   D   E

Question 18

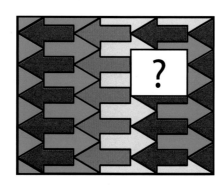

○   ○   ○   ○   ○
A   B   C   D   E

Question 19

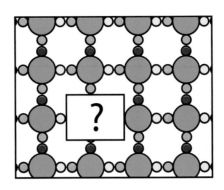

○ A   ○ B   ○ C   ○ D   ○ E

Question 20

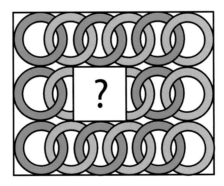

○ A   ○ B   ○ C   ○ D   ○ E

19

Question 21

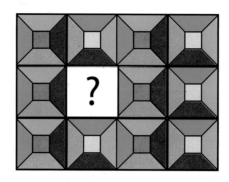

○ A   ○ B   ○ C   ○ D   ○ E

Question 22

○ A   ○ B   ○ C   ○ D   ○ E

Question 23

○   ○   ○   ○   ○
A   B   C   D   E

Question 24

○   ○   ○   ○   ○
A   B   C   D   E

Reasoning By Analogy

> **Directions:** In the reasoning by analogy section, look at the figures in the top row and determine how they are related. Choose the figure from the answer choices that goes with the figures in the bottom row in a similar way as shown in the top row.

Below is an example reasoning by analogy question:

Example

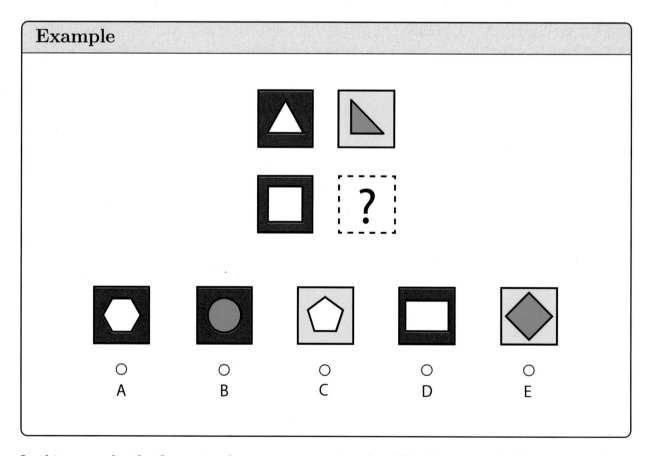

In this example, the figures in the top row are triangles. The figures in the bottom row have 4 sides. The figure in (E) is a blue 4-sided figure and is inside a yellow square. Therefore, (E) is the correct answer.

Question 1

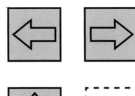

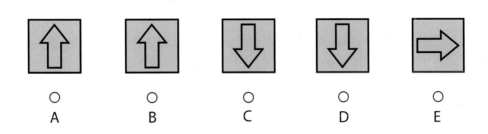

A	B	C	D	E

Question 2

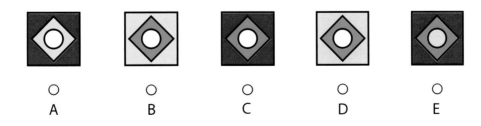

A	B	C	D	E

Question 3

○   ○   ○   ○   ○

A   B   C   D   E

Question 4

○   ○   ○   ○   ○

A   B   C   D   E

Question 5

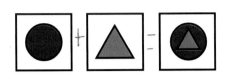

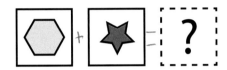

○   ○   ○   ○   ○
A   B   C   D   E

Question 6

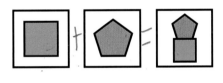

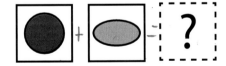

○   ○   ○   ○   ○
A   B   C   D   E

Question 7

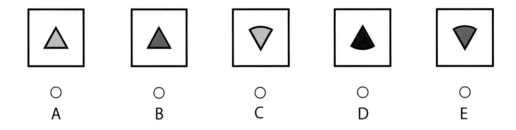

   A   B   C   D   E

Question 8

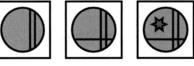

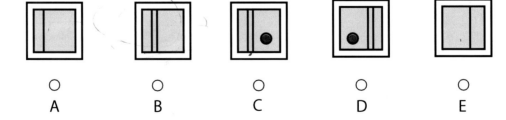

   A   B   C   D   E

Question 9

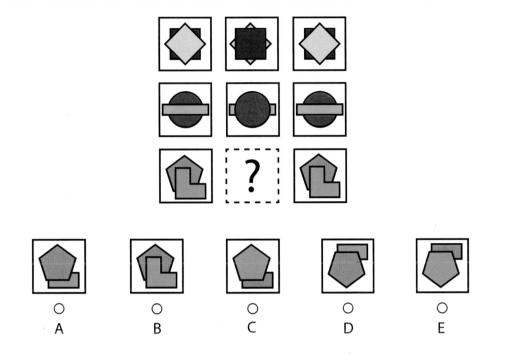

Question 10

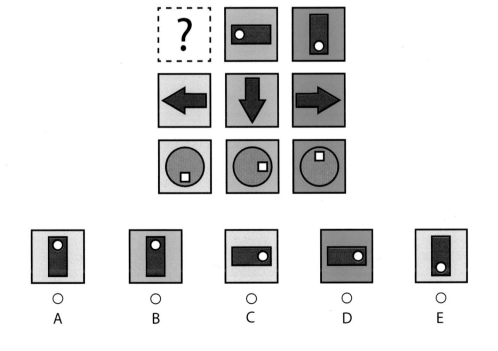

Question 11

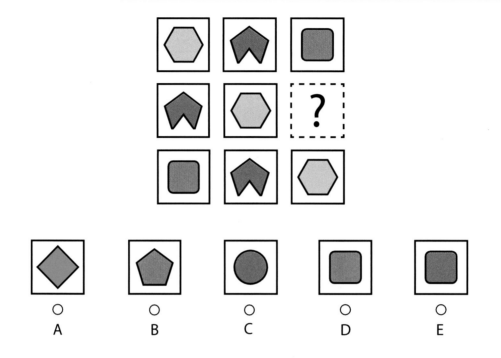

Question 12

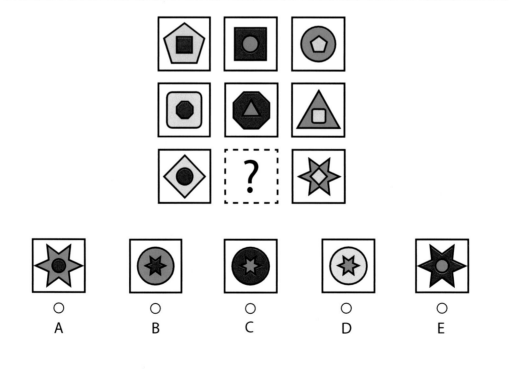

Serial Reasoning

Directions: In the serial reasoning section, each matrix is composed of nine boxes in a three-by-three grid. The figures changes as they go across the rows and down the columns of the matrix. Students will need to determine the patterns in the matrix and choose the figure from the answer choices that best completes the pattern.

Below is an example serial reasoning question:

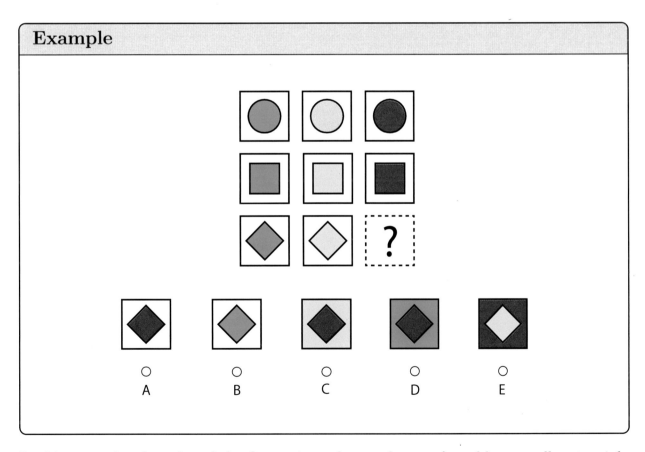

In this example, the color of the figures in each row changes from blue to yellow to pink. The figure in (A) is a pink diamond with white background. Therefore, (A) is the correct answer.

Question 1

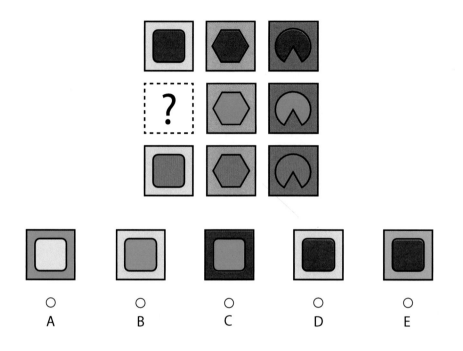

Question 2

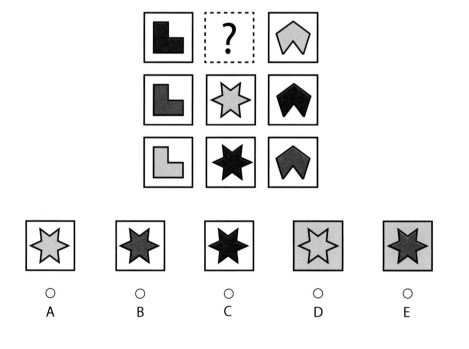

Question 3

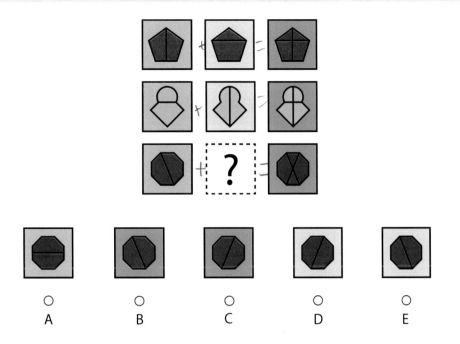

Question 4

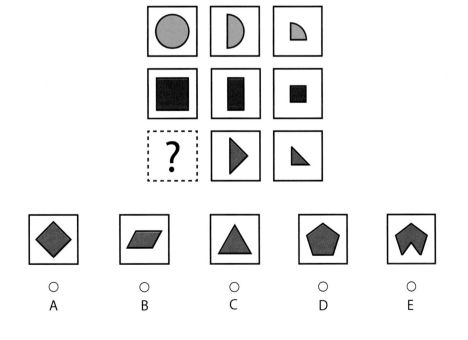

Question 5

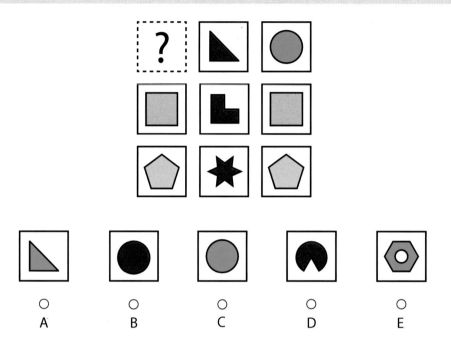

Question 6

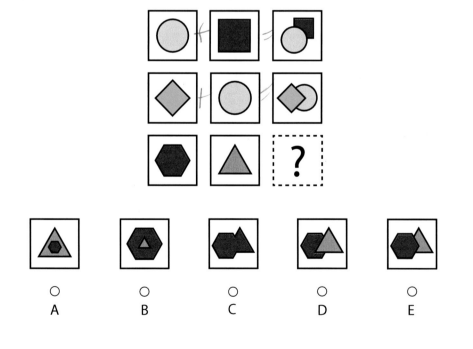

Question 7

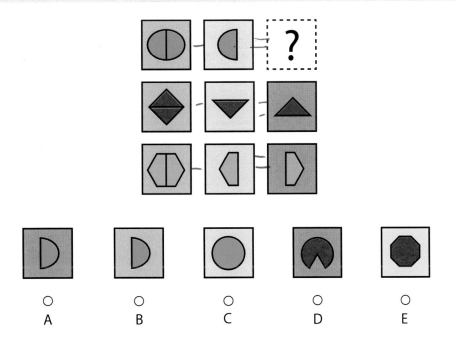

○ A   ○ B   ○ C   ○ D   ○ E

Question 8

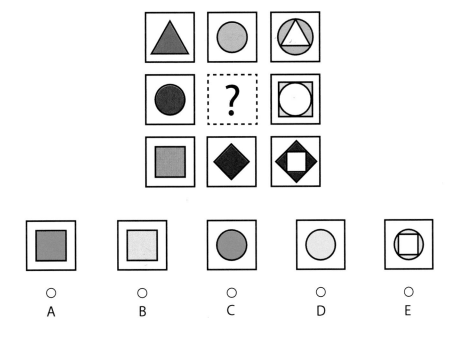

○ A   ○ B   ○ C   ○ D   ○ E

Question 9

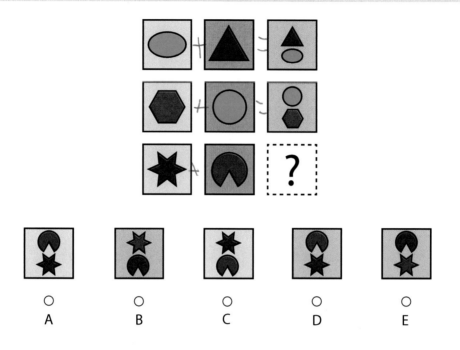

○   ○   ○   ○   ○

A   B   C   D   E

Question 10

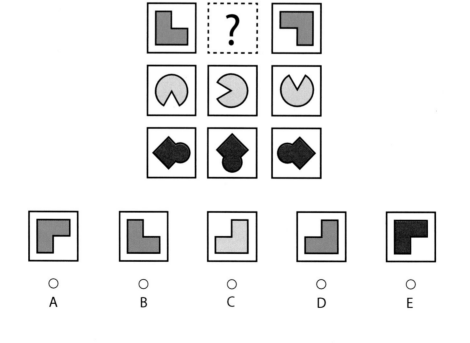

○   ○   ○   ○   ○

A   B   C   D   E

Question 11

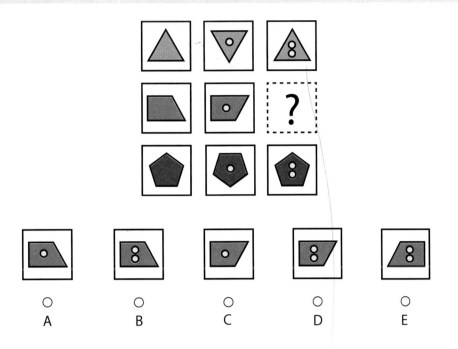

Question 12

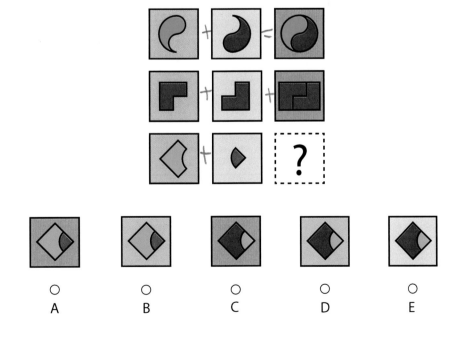

PRACTICE

TEST 2

Pattern Completion

Directions: In the pattern completion section, each question has a large rectangle with a design. There is a small rectangle with a question mark that hides part of the design. Choose the answer that best completes the design.

Below is an example pattern completion question:

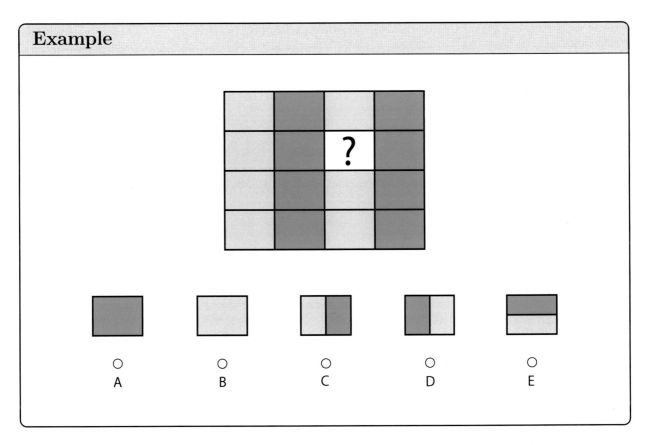

Example

In this example, the figure in (B) best completes the design. Therefore, (B) is the correct answer.

Question 1

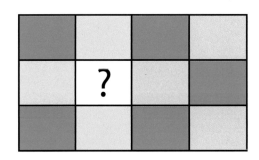

○   ○   ○   ○   ○
A   B   C   D   E

Question 2

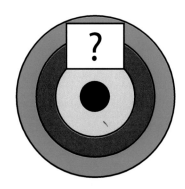

○   ○   ○   ○   ○
A   B   C   D   E

40

Question 3

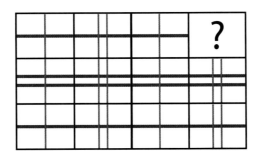

    ○   ○   ○   ○   ○
    A   B   C   D   E

Question 4

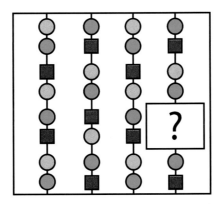

    ○   ○   ○   ○   ○
    A   B   C   D   E

Question 5

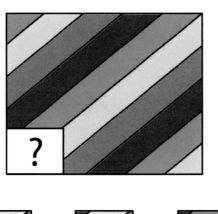

○ A   ○ B   ○ C   ○ D   ○ E

Question 6

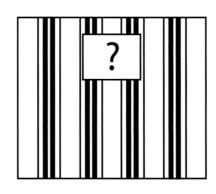

○ A   ○ B   ○ C   ○ D   ○ E

Question 7

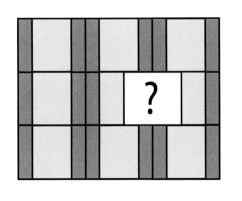

               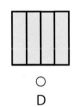

   ○   ○   ○   ○   ○
   A   B   C   D   E

Question 8

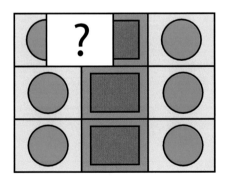

   ○   ○   ○   ○   ○
   A   B   C   D   E

Question 9

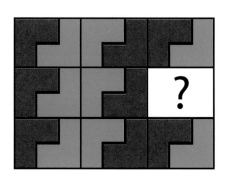

○   ○   ○   ○   ○
A   B   C   D   E

Question 10

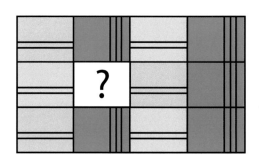

○   ○   ○   ○   ○
A   B   C   D   E

Question 11

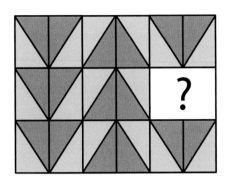

 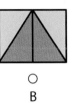

○ A ○ B ○ C ○ D ○ E

Question 12

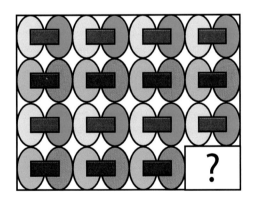

○ A ○ B ○ C ○ D ○ E

Question 13

○   ○   ○   ○   ○
A   B   C   D   E

Question 14

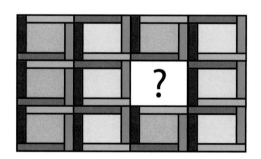

○   ○   ○   ○   ○
A   B   C   D   E

Question 15

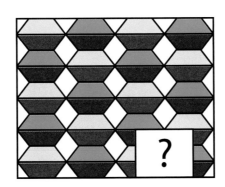

○ A 　 ○ B 　 ○ C 　 ○ D 　 ○ E

Question 16

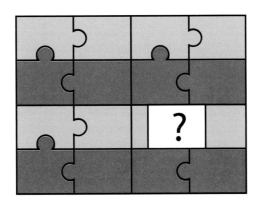

○ A 　 ○ B 　 ○ C 　 ○ D 　 ○ E

Question 17

   A   B   C   D   E

Question 18

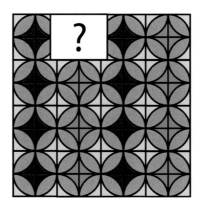

   A   B   C   D   E

Question 19

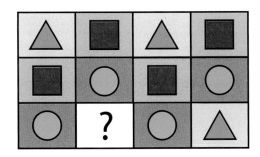

○   ○   ○   ○   ○
A   B   C   D   E

Question 20

○   ○   ○   ○   ○
A   B   C   D   E

Question 21

○   ○   ○   ○   ○
A   B   C   D   E

Question 22

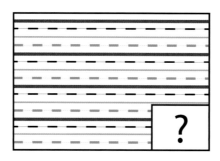

○   ○   ○   ○   ○
A   B   C   D   E

Question 23

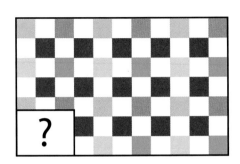

○   ○   ○   ○   ○
A   B   C   D   E

Question 24

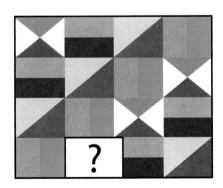

○   ○   ○   ○   ○
A   B   C   D   E

Reasoning By Analogy

Directions: In the reasoning by analogy section, look at the figures in the top row and determine how they are related. Choose the figure from the answer choices that goes with the figures in the bottom row in a similar way as shown in the top row.

Below is an example reasoning by analogy question:

Example

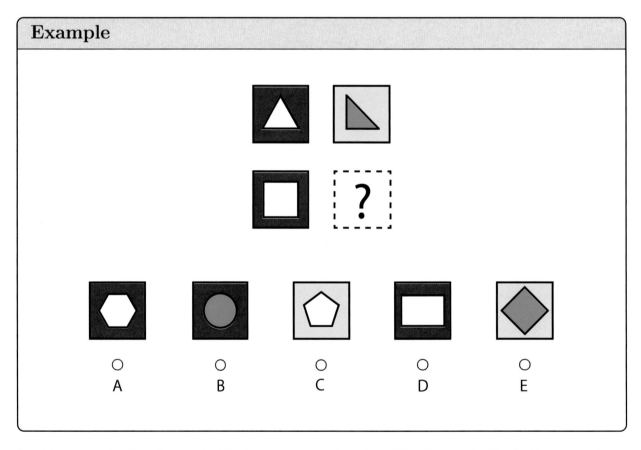

In this example, the figures in the top row are triangles. The figures in the bottom row have 4 sides. The figure in (E) is a blue 4-sided figure and is inside a yellow square. Therefore, (E) is the correct answer.

Question 1

○   ○   ○   ○   ○
A   B   C   D   E

Question 2

○   ○   ○   ○   ○
A   B   C   D   E

Question 3

○ A   ○ B   ○ C   ○ D   ○ E

Question 4

○ A   ○ B   ○ C   ○ D   ○ E

Question 5

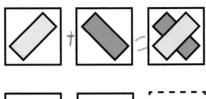

○   ○   ○   ○   ○

A   B   C   D   E

Question 6

 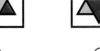

○   ○   ○   ○   ○

A   B   C   D   E

Question 7

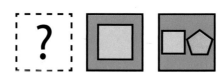

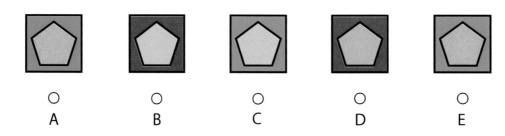

○ A   ○ B   ○ C   ○ D   ○ E

Question 8

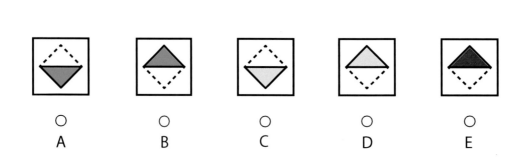

○ A   ○ B   ○ C   ○ D   ○ E

Question 9

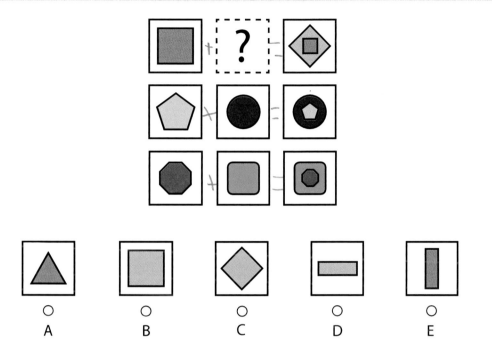

Question 10

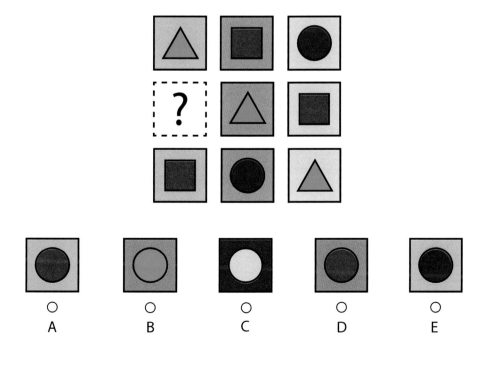

Question 11

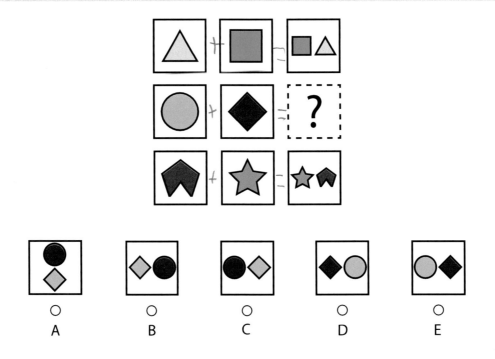

Question 12

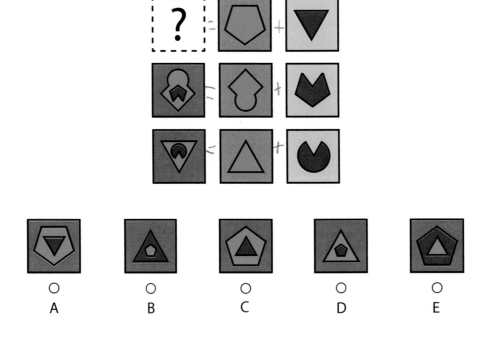

MR. RHEE'S BRILLIANT
MATH SERIES

Serial Reasoning

Directions: In the serial reasoning section, each matrix is composed of nine boxes in a three-by-three grid. The figures changes as they go across the rows and down the columns of the matrix. Students will need to determine the patterns in the matrix and choose the figure from the answer choices that best completes the pattern.

Below is an example serial reasoning question:

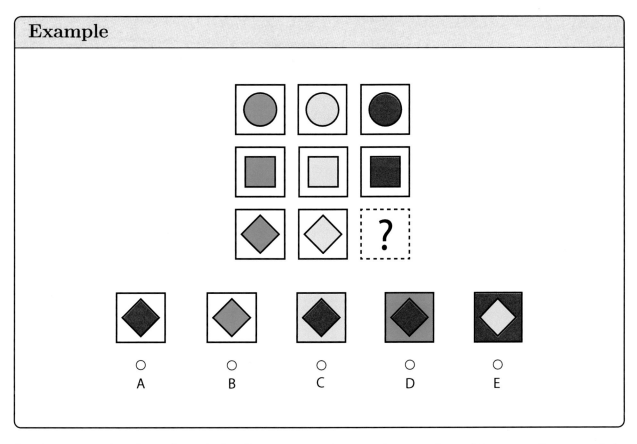

Example

In this example, the color of the figures in each row changes from blue to yellow to pink. The figure in (A) is a pink diamond with white background. Therefore, (A) is the correct answer.

Question 1

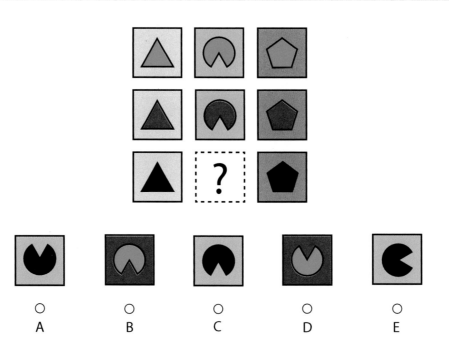

Question 2

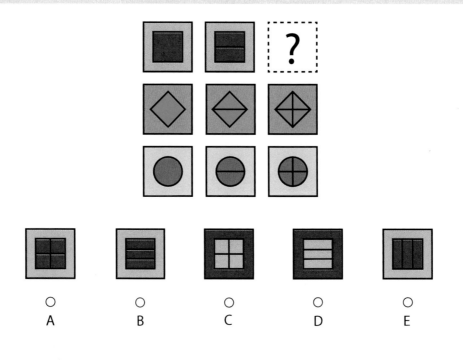

Question 3

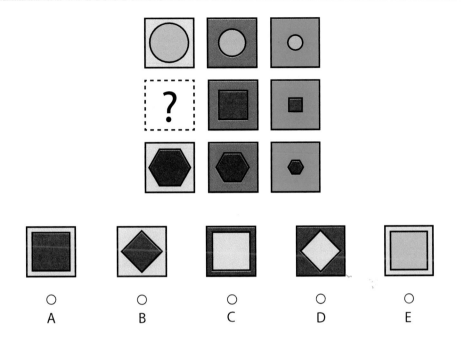

Question 4

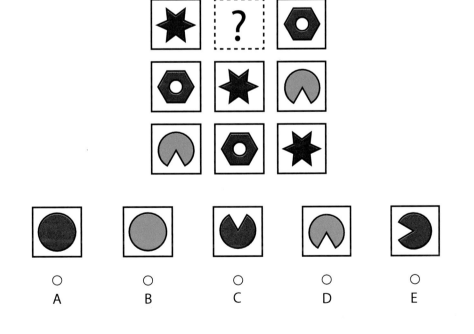

Question 5

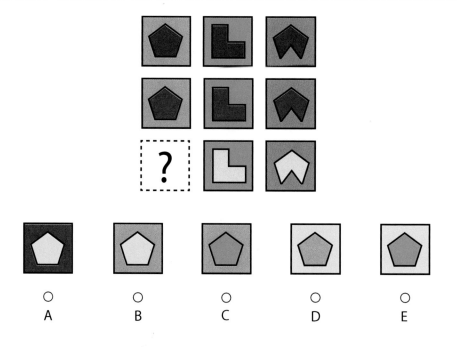

Question 6

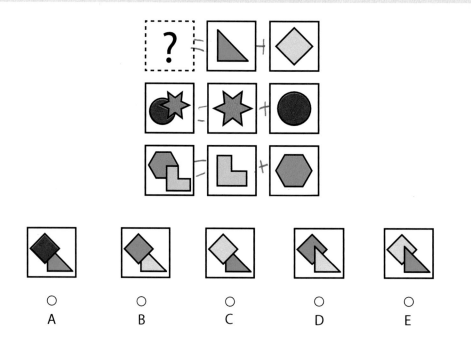

Question 7

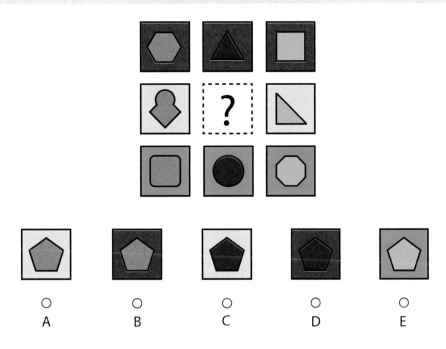

○ A   ○ B   ○ C   ○ D   ○ E

Question 8

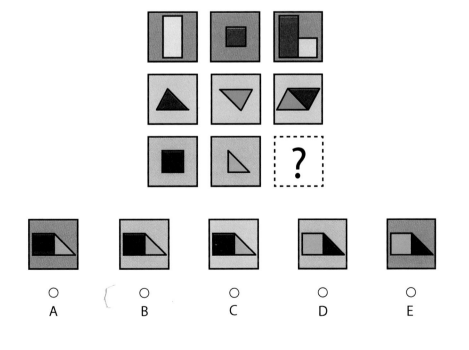

○ A   ○ B   ○ C   ○ D   ○ E

Question 9

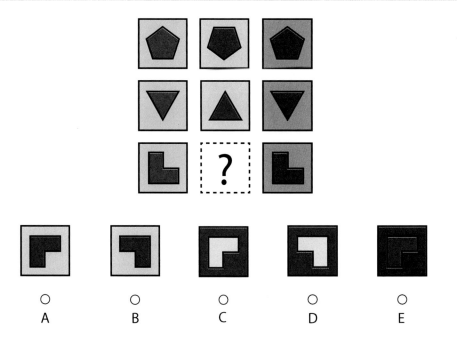

○ A   ○ B   ○ C   ○ D   ○ E

Question 10

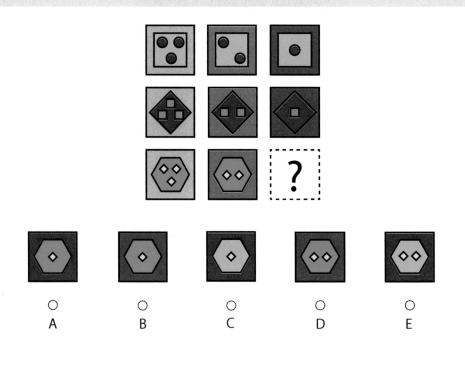

○ A   ○ B   ○ C   ○ D   ○ E

Question 11

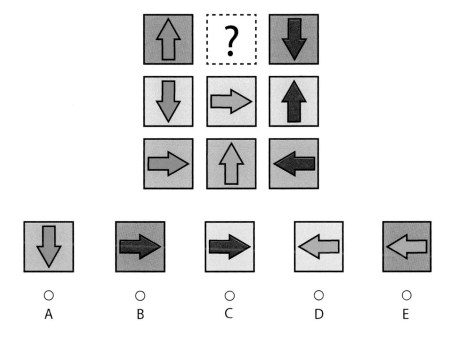

○ A   ○ B   ○ C   ○ D   ○ E

Question 12

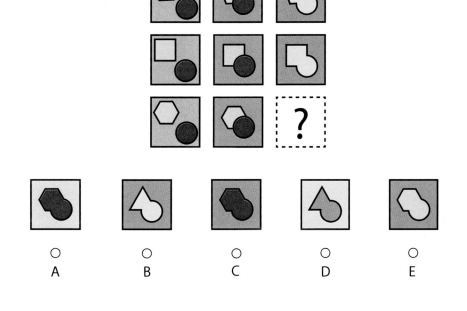

○ A   ○ B   ○ C   ○ D   ○ E

TEST 1 AND 2

ANSWERS

NNAT 2

Practice Test 1 Answers

Pattern Completion

1. C	6. E	11. E	16. E	21. B
2. A	7. D	12. C	17. E	22. C
3. A	8. E	13. D	18. E	23. B
4. A	9. A	14. B	19. A	24. B
5. E	10. D	15. D	20. C	

Reasoning By Analogy

1. D	6. A	11. D
2. C	7. E	12. C
3. E	8. B	
4. A	9. A	
5. E	10. A	

Serial Reasoning

1. B	6. E	11. B
2. B	7. A	12. A
3. D	8. B	
4. A	9. D	
5. C	10. A	

NNAT 2

Practice Test 2 Answers

Pattern Completion

1. E	6. B	11. D	16. C	21. C
2. D	7. A	12. E	17. B	22. C
3. B	8. C	13. D	18. A	23. D
4. C	9. A	14. A	19. E	24. B
5. D	10. B	15. B	20. E	

Reasoning By Analogy

1. D	6. B	11. D
2. C	7. E	12. C
3. A	8. B	
4. E	9. C	
5. C	10. E	

Serial Reasoning

1. C	6. C	11. E
2. A	7. C	12. E
3. A	8. D	
4. D	9. A	
5. B	10. B	

Made in the USA
Middletown, DE
07 November 2019

78133321R00040